PAWS
for
THOUGHT

MAUREEN MELVIN
Illustrations by Geoff Crook

CHAPMANS
1990

Chapmans Publishers Ltd
141-143 Drury Lane
London WC2B 5TB

BRITISH LIBRARY CATALOGUING IN PUBLICATION DATA

Melvin, Maureen
Paws for thought.
I. Title
821.914

ISBN 1-85592-506-0

First published by Chapmans

First reprint October 1991

Designed by Judy Linard
Typeset by Monoset (Typesetters) Ltd
Printed and bound in Great Britain by
The Bath Press, Avon

A ♥

N≈N

For
Nanette Newman
who had
faith in me.~

Introduction

Abigail is a tricolour Cavalier King Charles spaniel aged six.

She takes a great interest in current affairs and she is a keen television viewer, particularly of wildlife programmes.

Since she was a tiny puppy she has shown considerable literary ability and has celebrated various occasions, including the birthdays of her family and friends, in verse.

This is a small collection of her work, which she feels might be of interest to other dogs and their owners.

Author's Note

What do you know of a dog's life?
How much are you really aware
Of the intricate threads
That we weave in our heads
When you think we're asleep in the chair?

You know that we like to go hunting.
You know we are faithful and true.
But it may not be clear
That the dog you hold dear
Has a great deal in common with you.

You cannot have failed to observe us
As we pounce with a predatory paw
On the *Harpers & Queen*s
And the smart magazines
That you carelessly fling to the floor.

We keep a keen eye on the City,
Observing our stocks and our shares.
We like cricket and ballet,
Museums and the Hallé,
And programmes on current affairs.

If you follow my life and adventures
You may be astonished to find
That your four-legged friend
Stands revealed at the end
With a soul and a heart and a mind.

A Life in the Day of Abigail

My day begins at 6 a.m.
Commotion at the door –
The Times, the *Mail* and *Sporting Life*
Come hurtling to the floor.

I grip *The Times* between my teeth
And take it back to bed.
It's great they're all asleep upstairs,
And I'm one jump ahead.

And when I've scanned the headlines
And absorbed the crossword clues,
I skim across the hatched and matched
And see who's blown a fuse.

She comes downstairs at last, and we
Enjoy a blissful hug –
Two minutes' gay abandon
Every morning on the rug.

She gets involved with orange juice,
With porridge, toast and tea,
And if I play my cards right
There's a Farley's rusk for me.

With breakfast done, I'm outward bound
To start my dawn patrol.
Besides which, there's a limit
To my muscular control.

I like to test the morning air,
Especially when it snows
And every frosted blade of grass
Is nectar to my nose.

Then back inside and up to bed,
My favourite grandstand view,
To watch her while she paints her face
And sprays her hair with glue.

If I detect a sign that we're
About to hit the store,
I round up all the shopping bags
And hover by the door.

You need your wits about you
When you're walking in the town.
Stiletto heels and pushchair wheels
Conspire to mow you down.

I'm glad to pass the time of day
With hound or Labrador,
But little breeds of lesser size
I usually ignore.

At last the shopping bags are full –
And not a jot too soon.
We have to get home quickly
For I always dine at noon.

The menu often varies,
But it's always gourmet fare:
Spaghetti, pilchard fishcakes
Or a sirloin, medium rare.

And when I've had my forty winks
And downed some H_2O,
It's boots and coats and walking sticks,
And up the lane we go.

I always choose the daily route –
She doesn't seem to mind.
Besides, if I don't get my way
I only lag behind.

I put the breeze up rabbits,
But their fears they soon forget.
They know I'm only playing
And I haven't caught one yet.

I tiptoe through the pheasantry –
A dangerous pastime this.
The farmer has a shotgun
And he doesn't often miss.

It's safer out beyond the wood,
Across the open ground,
And I can run for miles and miles
With no one else around.

If we should meet the local hunt
I hide behind a tree.
I know they're looking for the fox,
I'm glad it isn't me.

The fox and I are faithful friends –
I have his home address.
I wouldn't leak it to the hounds
However hard they press.

My working day begins at four,
I'm not a parasite.
I sharpen all my pencils
And I settle down to write.

I only do an hour or two –
I find it very hard.
My spelling is disastrous
For a cultured canine bard.

And when I've reached my target,
If the hour is not too late,
I study the *Spectator*
Then I know I'm up to date.

I turn to Jeffrey Bernard,
Which means starting at the end,
But everyone begins with him –
He's everybody's friend.

I follow through the book reviews
And all the serious stuff.
By then my brain is reeling
And I know I've had enough.

It's time for relaxation
And I often have a snooze
Unless they're showing *Mastermind*,
The Meercats or the news.

It's lovely by the open fire,
The embers glowing red.
But all good things must have an end
And soon it's time for bed.

I do my late-night guard dog bit
With fearsome bark and growl,
Which petrifies the fieldmice
And infuriates the owl.

With half a rich tea biscuit
To sustain me through the night,
I settle on my beanbag,
And she switches off the light.

It must be quite apparent
That a dog needs lots of sleep,
Not just for chasing spectral cats
Or insubstantial sheep.

For we have 'clouds of glory' still
To trail around our heads.
And that is why we sleep so sound
And linger in our beds.

Some dogs win championships at Crufts,
Some never get to shine.
But every dog must have his day
And this, my friends, is mine.

Down in the Mouth

When Things Are Said about my breath
It is, of course, the kiss of death.
And just to make things harder yet
They whisk me off to see the vet.

I don't know why they take that tone.
At least my teeth are all my own.
I've never had a jacket crown
Like other dogs I've seen in town.

The vet and I are special chums.
I sit while he inspects my gums
And if I need a small repair
He straps me in the dentist's chair.

He tips me up from north to south
So he can see inside my mouth,
And with a powerful jet beneath
He cleans the tartar from my teeth.

I'm fairly good at sitting still
Until I hear that dreadful drill,
But if I kick and thrash about
A hypodermic puts me out.

And then I don't mind what they do
Until I wake up, good as new.
My gums are healthy, pink and bright
And all my teeth are shining white.

I rinse my mouth with pink champagne
And spit it smartly down the drain.
It's not a waste, it helps me find
The bits the dentist left behind.

Back on my feet, and down the High
I flash my teeth at passers-by,
And no one looks the other way.
I'm flavour of the month today!

A Sight for Sore Eyes

It's fun to chase the rabbits in the springtime,
And rustle through the barley field in May.
But I suffer from rhinitis
And severe conjunctivitis,
And my eyes and nose are streaming all the day.

It's the finest time to mix it with the wildlife.
There are pheasant, fox and guinea fowl to stalk.
But I need some special glasses
To protect me from the grasses,
So I'm off to buy some goggles for my walk.

Cats and Dogs

'It's raining cats and dogs,' they say.
I can't imagine why.
I've never noticed dogs and cats
Cascading from the sky.

Why don't they say, 'It's raining rats',
Or skunks, or ducks and drakes?
It could be raining crocodiles,
Or porcupines, or snakes.

I wish they'd follow my advice
And find a better phrase.
But man prefers the status quo
And hates to change his ways.

So when I'm dressed for action
In my Aquascutum togs,
'You can't go out today,' they'll say.
'It's raining cats and dogs.'

Ballerina

I wonder what I'd look like in a tutu.
I've practised my positions at the barre.
There'll be noses out of joint
When I pirouette on pointe
And they realize I'm an up-and-coming star.

I'll never be a prima ballerina,
But I'd like to be considered for the corps.
They could put me at the side
Till I get into my stride,
And I'll promise not to end up on the floor.

Swan Lake, of course, has always been my favourite,
And I'd love to have the chance of going on
In a modest little role,
Like a duckling or a mole,
'Cos I guess I'm not cut out to be a swan.

Christmas Dog

I'm not too keen on Christmas.
It's not the time for me,
With holly prickles under foot
And needles from the tree.

The house is pandemonium
And no one wants to play.
It doesn't matter where I go,
I'm always in the way.

I get a Christmas stocking,
Like the others in the house.
It's filled with chocolate buttons
And a tiny sugar mouse.

I think that Father Christmas
Ought to mind what he's about;
He stuffs them in so tightly
I can never get them out.

They dress me up in ribbons
And a silly paper hat.
They even call me 'Christmas Dog'–
I don't much care for that.

The Christmas message –'Peace on earth,
Goodwill to all mankind'–
Is bully for the human race,
The dog gets left behind.

If I could make a Christmas wish
Beneath the mistletoe,
I'd like to be in Bethlehem
Two thousand years ago

To watch beside the baby's crib –
The ox, the ass and me.
Now that's the kind of Christmas
I should really like to see.

The Straggler

The hunt was out last Monday,
Which was something of a bore.
They shut me in the kitchen
And secured the garden door.

I don't know why they fool around
With bolts and bars and locks.
I'd never even contemplate
A fracas with a fox.

The morning was a write-off
But my lunch was rather smart,
With scrambled egg and haddock,
And a slice of Bakewell tart.

We thought we'd take our usual stroll
Now all was quiet again,
So booted, spurred and fortified
We set off up the lane.

Our walk was interrupted
By a devastated dog,
Who must have swum the Channel
Or been stranded in a bog.

We asked him where he came from
But he hung his head in shame.
It seemed he'd been abandoned
With no collar and no name.

We had to take him with us –
He was done for, we could see.
I marched along by Mummy
And he limped along by me.

I offered him my drinking bowl
And tender cuts of meat.
He drank a little water
But was too upset to eat.

We sat together in the yard.
He couldn't come indoors –
I've never seen such dirty ears
And mud-encrusted paws.

I told him all about the hunt,
And tried to make it clear
It isn't right to chase the fox
Or shoot the Highland deer.

He turned, just once, towards me
And, though shabby and unkempt,
His glance, I felt, somehow concealed
A thinly veiled contempt.

Then, suddenly, the hunt was back,
The horses thundered past.
My new-found friend was on his feet,
His nerve restored at last.

He cleared the garden wall in one,
Then raced across the field.
I shuddered as the painful truth
Was finally revealed.

No disadvantaged vagrant this,
Escaping from the pound.
That dirty dog turned out to be
A bona fide hound.

The Spice of Life

I am well supplied with tins of beef and liver,
And they rustle up a lamb's heart when I wish,
But it's purely supposition
When those experts on nutrition
State that dogs like meat – and only cats like fish.

I once struck up a friendship with a moggie
Who would sell her soul for mince or sirloin steak.
And if anyone should doubt it
Let us make no bones about it,
I, myself, would kill for kippers, cod or hake.

But now the pet food boys have had a brainwave
And they've come up with a cracking good idea.
How I wish they'd done it sooner –
Tins of chicken laced with tuna –
And discriminating dogs will raise a cheer!

Royal Dogs

I've never met a corgi,
They're not as royal as me
Although they're always out in force
Where royalty choose to be.

They haven't got a charter
To raise them from the ranks.
They can't drop in to swimming pools,
To theatres, shops or banks.

I have it from the horse's mouth
They snap at ladies' feet,
And other things have come to light
I'd rather not repeat.

No doubt they're in the running
For an edict of their own.
I guess they think they've got it made
With one foot on the throne.

They'll have to pull their socks up
And mind their p's and q's.
You don't win royal appointments
By destroying people's shoes.

Perhaps they should remember
The title 'Royal' is mine.
King Charles bestowed it long ago
And I'm the first in line.

Featherweight

My hunting skills are all revealed
When chasing feathers in the field.
The birds obligingly divest
Themselves of plumage from the nest,
And all their cast-off debris flies
And drifts and floats before my eyes.
Then I can leap into the air
And snap up feathers everywhere.

One morning when the wind was high
A lady, who was riding by,
Pulled up to watch my expertise
With wayward feathers in the breeze.

Now, as a rule, I'm not aware
Of anyone who stops to stare.
This lady, though, the forward kind,
Called out to see if we would mind
Her coming in to ask my name.
I knew she'd interrupt my game,

But manners maketh dog, I feel,
And came obediently to heel.

She studied me from head to toe,
And we were most relieved to know
The reason for the third degree –
She'd had a little dog like me.

This Henrietta, we were told –
A sporting type, just nine years old –
Had been out rabbiting for hours
And must have overtaxed her powers.
She ate her dinner, drank her drink,
Then to the garden room to sink
Exhausted on the cold stone floor,
She gave a cry and breathed no more.
We voiced our sympathy, of course,
To both the lady and the horse,
Suggesting, as we reached the gate,
Perhaps the dog was overweight.
The lady eyed my well-filled fur.
'Not half', she said 'as fat as *her*.'

And with this shattering display
She wheeled her horse and rode away.

We plodded home with solemn tread.
No smiles were smiled, no words were said.
Once safely back, I crept inside
And tried to find a place to hide.
I wedged myself behind a chair,
I didn't stick out anywhere.
When tea-time came she didn't call –
No chocolate bones for me at all.

And later, in a dismal heap
I sobbed my portly self to sleep.

Next morning I recovered fast,
Determined to forget the past
And keep my friends and critics quiet
By following a rigid diet.
I'd buy myself a set of weights,
Some boxing gloves and roller skates.
I'd exercise and swim and jog
And be a snake-hipped, slimline dog.

St Abb's Head

There's a headland on the south-east coast of Scotland,
Almost midway between Berwick and Dunbar.
It stands high above the sea
And they named it after me,
And it's known to every self-respecting tar.

St Abb's Head is a most important landmark,
And you'll hear it mentioned nearly every day
As they warn the deep-sea sailors
To stand ready with their bailers
When a gale-force wind is rising in the bay.

I always like to catch the shipping forecast,
And to hear my name go winging through the air
Though they've spelt me rather quaint –
Still, it's nice to be a saint
With a weather eye on shipping everywhere.

BBC Points of View

I don't suppose you get much mail
From little dogs like me.
I'm so upset, I had to write
And tell the BBC.

I waited all the week to see
Some coverage of the show –
The championship at Crufts, I mean,
In case you didn't know.

The only programme I could find
Was late on Sunday night
When royalist Cavalier King Charles
Like me are tucked up tight.

I stayed up late to see who won
But got no satisfaction.
They gave it to an Airedale
Of Italian extraction!

Please will you ask the powers that be
To give us all a break,
And show the championship for dogs
While dogs are still awake!

Best of Friends

You'll recall my friend The Straggler whom I wrote about before –
He's the hound we found abandoned up the lane.
Well, he soon regained his *joie de vivre* and joined the hunt once more,
And I never thought our paths would cross again.

I was playing by the railway bridge one crisp November day,
Chasing rabbits, though it's strictly out of bounds,
When the fox appeared from nowhere and went swiftly on his way
Followed closely by the huntsmen and the hounds.

They streamed across the open field towards the aerodrome
And I stayed quite still, unnoticed by the pack.
I was just about to make a dash for freedom and for home
When I spotted an obstruction on the track.

I crept a little closer – the embankment was so steep
And it seemed an endless distance to the ground –
But before I lost my footing and made one last desperate leap
I had seen the mystery object was a hound!

I didn't stop to think as I went tumbling down the hill
In a mass of prickles, feathers, leaves and mud.
I could only see him lying there so helpless and so still,
Then I landed on the railway with a thud.

I knew there was no time to lose, but what was I to do
For at any moment now there'd be a train?
And the hound who lay abandoned and whose lips were turning blue
Was my friend The Straggler, grounded once again.

He must have been unconscious for his eyes were tightly shut
And I tried the kiss of life to no avail.
He lay twisted, torn and bleeding and his head was badly cut,
And his injured paw was resting on the rail.

I didn't have much faith in the impression I might make,
But I braced myself and heaved with all my might.
I'd made hardly any headway when the rails began to shake
And the Cheltenham Flyer thundered into sight.

Our time was up. I heaved once more, I thought my lungs would burst,
Then The Straggler moved and rolled beside the track.
But the monster was upon us and about to do his worst
When I tripped and fell and everything went black.

It's strange, but when I came alive my memory was a blank.
I was overcome by weariness and pain.
Then I saw The Straggler carried on a stretcher up the bank
And the dreadful scene came back to me again.

There were lots of people round me as I struggled to my feet
But I couldn't walk, my legs were stiff and sore.
So a kindly stranger lifted me and wrapped me in a sheet
Then he drove me home and dropped me at my door.

There was bound to be an inquest, I was really in a spot
For the railway bridge has always been taboo.
Still, I wasn't out for compliments – a hero I am not
And I only did what any dog would do.

There was talk about 'ungrateful dogs' and 'those who've gone astray',
But she bathed my feet and stroked my aching head.
I enjoyed a bowl of porridge – I'd had nothing else all day –
Then I staggered in a stupor into bed.

It was ages till I heard the news, a week or even more,
When a message came especially for me
That the convalescent Straggler wished to even up the score
And requested that I visit him for tea.

And that is how it happened that we drove in through the gate
Of a country house I'd never seen before.
It was plain to see The Straggler lived in unexpected state
With a coat of arms above the stable door.

We had a simply marvellous feast, with scrambled egg on toast
And a dish of tea, undoubtedly Earl Grey.
And when we'd cleared the decks it was suggested by my host
That I join him for a gossip in the hay.

The next two hours were riveting. I hung on every word
For The Straggler was an awesome raconteur,
And his exploits and adventures were the best I'd ever heard –
I was stiff with cramp but too engrossed to stir.

The stable clock struck six and it was time for me to go,
And I thanked him as I started for the door.
But when I proposed a meeting in another week or so
He just looked at me and raised a bandaged paw.

I didn't fret, I knew there'd be some splendid times ahead
And my life went on exactly as before.
Then I dreamed one night The Straggler came and stood beside my bed,
And explained we couldn't visit any more.

He realized he was failing and his hunting days were through,
So he'd travelled to a country far away
Where unwanted dogs are welcomed, and rejuvenated, too.
But he couldn't take me with him, sad to say.

When I woke up in the morning I remembered what he'd said,
And I knew he was one cheerful happy hound.
He'd looked bright and young and handsome with no stitches in his head
And his legs were mended straight and firm and sound.

The Straggler was my faithful friend. I'm sad he's gone away,
Though he'll interrupt my dreams from time to time.
I suppose there's nothing for it when a dog has had his day
So I'm taking steps to linger in my prime.

Hospitality

I had a friend to stay last week –
It wasn't a success –
A grand Old English sheepdog,
But, my goodness, what a mess!

You couldn't see her eyes for hair,
She didn't even look
When I pointed out the pictures
In my favourite poetry book.

I tried to make her welcome,
I could see that she was shy.
I told her tales of shaggy dogs
But all she did was cry.

She wouldn't touch her dinner
So I offered to help out,
But that idea went down like lead
Since I'm a trifle stout.

I showed her round the garden
And I took her up the lane.
She found the usual offices
Then lumbered back again.

She commandeered my beanbag –
I don't think that was right.
She fell asleep and never stirred;
I counted sheep all night.

She went away next morning.
I didn't feel the loss.
This, clearly, is a one-dog house
And, clearly, I'm the boss!

Heartache

I fell in love with a Labrador
When I was only three.
He would often stroll by the garden gate
In the evenings after tea.

He always gave me a friendly nod
And passed the time of day,
But he never touched me nose to nose
Or asked me out to play.

I saved him crispy pieces of fish
And chocolate bones from tea,
But I understood what I felt for him
Was not what he felt for me.

One day he came with a jaunty step
And a lady by his side.
She was truly a golden Labrador
And destined to be his bride.

My heart sank down to the tip of my tail
When I saw the way things were.
I gave him my finest chocolate bone
But he laid it in front of her.

I saw him rarely after that
And I think he moved away,
But I used to wait by the garden gate
When the sun went down each day.

I never fell in love again,
And nobody fell for me,
For I lost my heart to a Labrador
When I was only three.

Something in the City

for my friend Nick

I know you're very witty
And you're 'something in the city',
Although no one ever tells me what you do.
So I thought you might be willing
To assist me with a shilling,
Then I'd come along and spend the day with you.

When you leave the subway station
At your usual destination
I'll be keeping close behind you in the crush.
And I hope you won't outstrip me
For there's quite a lot to trip me,
With my brolly and my briefcase and my brush.

It will all be most exciting –
I'll be adding up and writing,
And I'll master things I never knew before.
When it's clear that I'm not swanking,
Just a whizz at corporate banking,
Then your friends will want to shake me by the paw.

And at lunchtime we'll go walking
If you're not too busy talking,
And we'll call in at a sandwich bar or two.
But if business is too pressing
We'll stay in and keep them guessing
With a steak for me and strawberries for you.

As the afternoon advances
I'll consolidate my chances
In a bid for quick promotion to the board.
But the speedy circulation
Of my canine inspiration
Will ensure that all the profits will have soared.

When the day is nearly ended,
And our homeward way we've wended,
Then we'll grab a Chinese take-away for two.
And we'll sit in your pagoda
With a well-earned Scotch and soda,
And I'll be a merchant banker, just like you.

A Birthday Card For Daddy

I wanted to buy you this picture
As a present from Mummy and me.
But the Wallace Collection
Agreed on reflection
They couldn't take ninety-five p.

So we went to the shop that sells postcards
And we found you a copy instead.
And I'm happy to say
I was able to pay
Without putting myself in the red.

If you searched through the Louvre or Uffizi
You couldn't do better than that,
And I think you'll agree
It's the image of me
With my feather, my coat and my hat!

Soul Searching

I'm going to be an angel
When my life on earth is done.
I'm going to fly around the sky
And shine on everyone.

I don't pay much attention
To that silly rigmarole
That dogs don't go to heaven
'Cos they haven't got a soul.

Well, Mummy thinks I've got one,
And she's very often right.
She always says, 'God bless you'
When she tucks me in at night.

I've made a few enquiries
And that theory's full of holes.
There's someone up in Kemble Wood
Who stocks immortal souls.

It's my old friend the badger.
He's as clever as can be.
He stores them all in boxes
In a fallen chestnut tree.

You can't just go and buy one,
You have to pass the test,
Like helping toads across the road
Or birds to build their nest.

You have to rescue waifs and strays,
(I've done my share of that)
And learn to nod politely
When confronted by the cat.

I think I'll keep it under wraps
So no one else will know.
I'll pack it in my travelling bag
And take it when I go.

The soul will be my passport
But I'll need a few more things:
I'll have to ask St Francis
For a halo and some wings.

And when I've mastered miracles,
And earned some free weekends,
I'll hover over Gloucestershire
And wave to all my friends.